JUDGEMENT DAY

POEMS FOR A NEW WORLD

JUDGE THE POET

JUDGEMENT DAY

Copyright © 2022 Judge The Poet

All rights reserved.

ISBN: 9798361992812

JUDGEMENT DAY

FOR

CME, SOR AND ADR

Judge

JUDGE THE POET

JUDGEMENT DAY

CONTENTS

1	Into The Light	Pg 3
2	Snow	Pg 5
3	Poems	Pg 7
4	When I Awoke	Pg 9
5	Loss	Pg 11
6	The Abuse Of Fame	Pg 13
7	Everyday	Pg 15
8	Haircuts	Pg 17
9	Death	Pg 19
10	To –	Pg 21
11	Television	Pg 23
12	The Pessimist	Pg 25
13	The Planet	Pg 27
14	The Optimist	Pg 29
15	Feelings	Pg 31
16	The Glory Of The Game	Pg 33

17	Armed Struggle	Pg 35
18	Hidden Racism	Pg 37
19	Poetry	Pg 39
20	The Rainforest	Pg 41
21	Another Civil War	Pg 45
22	Destination	Pg 47
23	Art	Pg 49
24	The Shriek	Pg 51
25	What Is Love?	Pg 53
26	A Perfect Life?	Pg 55
27	Chasing Shadows	Pg 57
28	Babies	Pg 59
29	Love	Pg 61
30	The Cage Of Fire	Pg 63
31	The Shopper	Pg 65
32	The Candle	Pg 67
33	Developing Nation	Pg 69
34	Roses	Pg 71
35	The Rhythm Of Bali	Pg 73

36	The Chosen Way	Pg 77
37	The Martyr	Pg 79
38	Nature	Pg 81
39	Logic	Pg 83
40	The Family	Pg 85
41	Civilisation	Pg 87
42	Dream Weaver	Pg 89
43	My Friend	Pg 91
44	Habit	Pg 93
45	For –	Pg 95
46	When? Where? How?	Pg 97
47	Yesterday	Pg 99
48	The Village	Pg 101
49	Now	Pg 103
50	The Volcano	Pg 105
51	Money	Pg 107
52	Newborn	Pg 109
53	Big Business	Pg 111
54	Teenagers	Pg 113

JUDGEMENT DAY

55	Dawn	Pg 115
56	To The Politician	Pg 117
57	Elephants	Pg 119
58	Sex	Pg 121
59	And Now	Pg 123
60	Pleasantly Bored	Pg 125
61	Question And Answer	Pg 127
62	Dreams	Pg 129
63	New World	Pg 131
64	Two Rules	Pg 133
65	One Nation	Pg 135

JUDGEMENT DAY

JUDGEMENT DAY

There are three different styles of poem within this collection:

A. PERFORMANCE POETRY
   Street, stage, screen;

B. BRAINDROPS
   Short, provocative, inspiring;

C. REFLECTIONS
   Further, other thoughts.

JUDGEMENT DAY

JUDGEMENT DAY

Into The Light

A blazing light burns inside every soul -
To find and share that light is the purest goal.
And such endeavours provide their own reward
Until the world discovers the treasure it hoards.

For our challenge is to discover what we can be
And reveal the fullest potential of our destiny.
Let us improve what we can as we pass along
And simply leave the world a little less wrong.

Too many try to put obstacles in our way:
"You cannot be so naïve," they naïvely say,
"It is never that simple. That cannot be right.
Please stay in the dark… ignore the light."

Yet the sun shines so brightly there outside,
Showing beautiful sights from which we can't hide.
Choose to make the change. Cross that threshold.
Let all the beauty and sense fully unfold…

JUDGEMENT DAY

JUDGEMENT DAY

Snow

The snow landed

Softly.

Birds sang

Loudly,

As if trying to keep warm.

The door opened.

A little boy

Emerged,

Wrapped comfortably

Against the cold.

'Reality'

Thought the boy,

Without even knowing

He was thinking it,

'Is a beautiful thing.'

And then

He played all afternoon.

JUDGEMENT DAY

Poems

Poems are silly... Poems are dumb...
Poems are just little ditties to hum.
It all seems so stupid, seems so absurd:
Putting your thoughts in a few pretty words!

Who needs that rhythm? Who needs that sound?
There's enough songs and slogans going around.
Poems can't say what I think, what I feel...
Isn't it time for something a little more real?

But look! I've done it... Put my thoughts in rhyme.
So much was expressed in so little time.
Perhaps I was wrong. It wasn't so bad.
Maybe all poets aren't pretentious or mad.

That cannot be right. I've always been sure
That poems are dull - a waste and a bore.
I thought it was stupid... thought it absurd;
But I just put my thoughts in a few pretty words.

JUDGEMENT DAY

When I Awoke

When I awoke,
I'd forgotten who I was.

Forgotten
Who to hate.
Forgotten
Which flag to love,
Kill and die for.

I'd forgotten
My separate language.
Animals called,
Trees whispered,
As if for me.

I felt alive,
At one with my planet.

One day,
Will we all
Wake like this?

JUDGEMENT DAY

Loss

The future is not about forgetting the past...
It's taking treasured memories and making them last.
And strength and love can help you recall
The earlier devotion and wonder of it all.

When we feel deep emptiness we try to cope;
Striving for reasons while longing for hope.
And though comfort can feel distant from our distress,
Love lives beyond sight and sound, never the less.

When new flowers bloom we sense love and glory,
Like when a child smiles at his grandmother's story;
And then we know the strength will surely come through
To help us nurture all of these beauties so new.

For the future is not about forgetting the past...
It's taking treasured memories and making them last.
And strength and love can help you recall
The true devotion and wonder of it all.

Sometimes the day's end can break your heart...
But elsewhere the same sun must find a new start.

JUDGEMENT DAY

The Abuse of Fame

A bankrupt tycoon goes on trial...
Arriving in Rolls Royce with a broad smile.
Some politicians believe whatever they do
Is above our range and out of our view.

Another hero's wrongs are found out;
"It couldn't be!" goes up the shout...
It's hard to watch your idols slipping
After hopeful years of blind worshipping.

Another 'star', we find, is nothing but a fraud;
Of all of this I am so very bored.
They seem to believe their fame supplies
Magic blinding glitter before our eyes.

Do they think they have nothing to fear
While they're 'up there' and we're 'down here'?
Well, I say: "There is no bottom, there is no top.
And the abuse of fame... it has to stop."

JUDGEMENT DAY

JUDGEMENT DAY

<u>Everyday</u>
Simple pleasures
Stir the same
Feelings
As grand moments.

Gently
And more slowly.

The gradual drip
Drip
Of realisation
And experience

Builds up
To a fountain
Of joy.

Thinly spread
Treasure,
Hiding in an ocean
Of normality.

JUDGEMENT DAY

Haircuts

What to do with the hair on your head?
A short-back-and-sides? Maybe some dreads?
Perhaps an ageing actor's steely wig?
Or something bouffant and very big?

To wear it casual or to wear it formal?
Dare to be different or pretend to be normal?
To part at the side or part at centre?
Should you consult a haircut inventor?

A presidential blow-wave you could wear
To show you're strong but show you care.
Slicked back, greased up, big or tiny...
Bleached, peroxide, matt or shiny...

A pony-tail you could learn to like...
A thousand curls or a single red spike...
Well, here's the answer - if you dare:
Do what you want, it's your hair!

JUDGEMENT DAY

JUDGEMENT DAY

<u>Death</u>

When I die,

How shall they

Speak of me?

Time waster

Or time user?

My efforts

Are the same. Only

The outcome

Is indefinite.

My deeds

Are my deeds.

The result

Is

Indivisible.

JUDGEMENT DAY

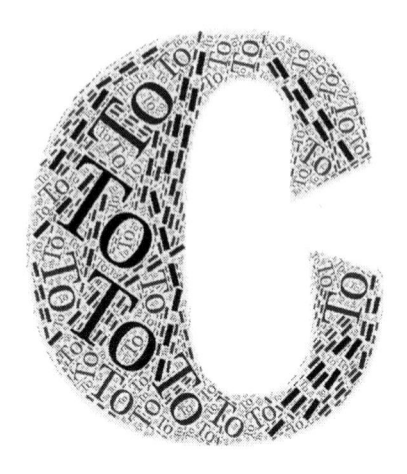

JUDGEMENT DAY

<u>To -</u>

There is honey melting within her eyes;
She is an angel in beautiful disguise.
Her lips are sweet and fresh like dew,
Her spirit shines out gentle and true.

The special soul she holds inside
Pours through her body and cannot hide;
The warmth of touch and tender hand
Are a glory to feel and understand.

For all my life I've sought the one
Whose spirit shone out like the sun;
And the strength of light I am now seeing
Outshines every other human being.

These are not words; they're facts I know.
They're just some of the reasons I love you so.
Be sure your beauty - both inside and out -
For me are beyond all possible doubt.

Let our destinies entwine so you may say
You'll be truly loved and valued every day...

JUDGEMENT DAY

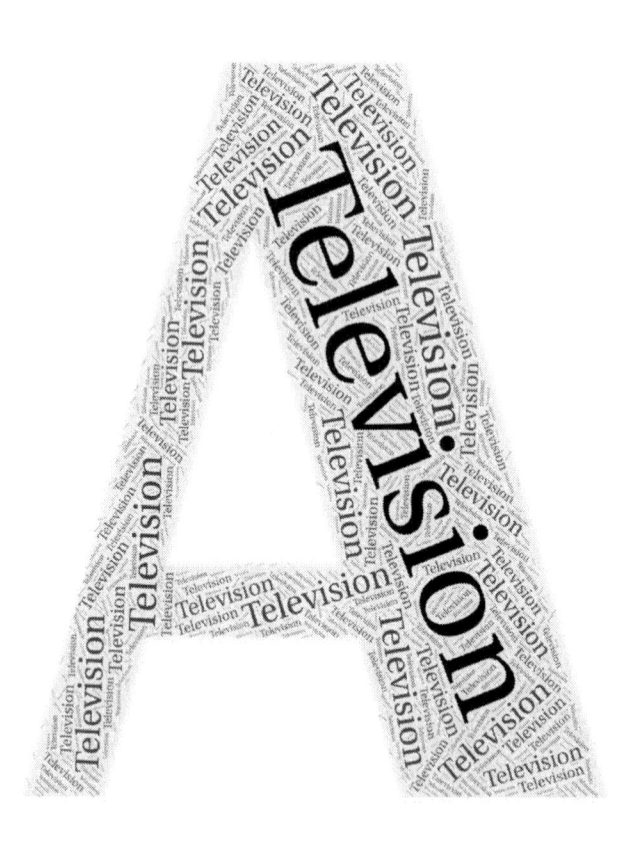

Television

One fact, of course, we know is true...
Without TV we'd have nothing to do.
And who would really want to move
Once you're into that TV groove...?

Fast action, great violence, bright cartoons;
Adverts flash by with such happy tunes.
The news is bright, flash and glary too...
What were those stories? Were they true?

Oh look! It's that famous whats-a-name!
Taking part in a riotous new quiz game!
Are these repeats? You think so? Might be.
All the programmes look the same to me.

Sometimes with TV I feel such frustration -
To show it I actually change the station.
But mostly I know my life is whole...
With the couch, the box and remote control.

JUDGEMENT DAY

The Pessimist

A purple patch

Can catch

A dream.

But black

Is my colour.

JUDGEMENT DAY

The Planet

Sometimes people wonder what we would find
If we thought not of Us and Them, but of Humankind.
Just imagine the things we would tolerate no more...
Like starvation and hatred, poverty and war.

But sometimes the idea comes into my mind,
Suppose we talked about all Planetkind.
Oceans and forests no longer playgrounds for our wishes;
We'd have to consider animals, trees, plants and fishes.

Just imagine the whole planet working as one,
Us using our powers like a world guardian.
Isn't this exactly how our future should be deployed?
A choice between global family and planet destroyed.

Big business, no doubt, will think the idea is mad.
Cynics will scoff and say we're naïve and sad.
But let's start a petition, stating: "We, the undersigned,
Won't talk of Us, Them or It... but of all Planetkind."

JUDGEMENT DAY

The Optimist

The sun shines

For me.

The moon waxes

And wanes

According to my movements.

Dreams are the map.

Travel with me.

JUDGEMENT DAY

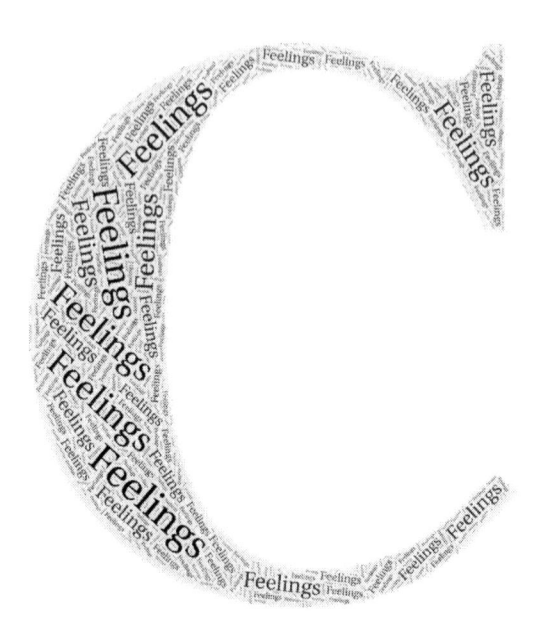

JUDGEMENT DAY

Feelings

Life, I find,
Like angled cobwebs,
Entangles in my eyes.
But through the haze
I feel the ways
We live and love and die.

Why must I feel
Each passing day,
More futile than the first,
Is new or old,
Better or good,
But never never worst?

Must we pass on
To see what comes
And make the best of it?
To feel, to touch,
To have, to hold
And never question it?

We feel to die
And that is why
Our feelings are ashamed,
As we pass on
Through thick and thin
Not daring to be named

Nor asked the question: "Why?"

JUDGEMENT DAY

The Glory of the Game

The players can earn money you would not believe;

No wonder they're willing to cheat and deceive.

Greed and ego - what a team… what a farce…

The winning comes first and the playing comes last.

Please pick a side - you just have to choose.

But, of course, I will kill you if my side lose.

Dividing nations and cities - creating a schism:

The glory of sport reduced to… racism.

Now sport could be such a positive thing -

With the joy and challenge that it can bring.

Seeing human achievement at its best:

Mind and body surviving every test.

So let the greedy go jump, the egos be out,

The aggressive and brainless be down for the count.

Can't we bring back the glory, bring back the art?

Let's make this happen - with today as the start.

JUDGEMENT DAY

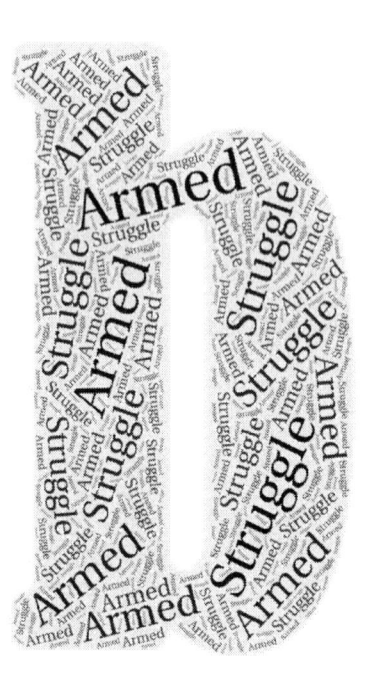

Armed Struggle

War is a whore

Sorry politicians

Climb aboard

With relish.

Other people's children

Die

According to their fantasies.

Masturbation

Would be better.

JUDGEMENT DAY

A Hidden Racism

Hidden Racism

Some politicians, and others, use elegant smiles
To hide their racism... which otherwise reviles.
They don't admit their evil in case we misjudge it:
Hiding hatred of skin-colour with "concerns for the budget".

Their ignorance and stupidity are always around,
Concealed with despicable and well-crafted sounds.
Some make jokes and slurs – but it's only in "fun"
... A humour that can kill more than any gun.

Racism often is hidden – it's the coward's game.
All humans, we know, are fundamentally the same.
And our world could exist as a beautiful mix;
But evil can destroy it with contemptible tricks.

So let's unite and be strong, letting all people know
That the only sane way for our future to go
Is with everyone together. Each working for all.
It's the challenge to which we must rise, not fall.

JUDGEMENT DAY

Poetry

Poetry is tosh?

I love tosh.

Tosh can be important.

JUDGEMENT DAY

JUDGEMENT DAY

The Rainforest: A Gallery Of Life

Gallery entry is free. But open only to the gentlest request...
This stirring example of evolving beauty at its very best
Where the richest secrets of nature are constantly confessed.
Golden light combines, like jigsaw pieces, with the deepest of jade
To cover this timeless universe wherein is faultlessly displayed
A majestic infinity of creations - of every dimension and shade.
Ancient trees entwine and cascade, purposefully striving to mark
The territory they must control with their leaf, root and bark,
Housing countless birds and animals, by day and by dark.
A vibrant catalogue including ferns, palms and pine
Nurtures generations of fruits and flowers of kaleidoscopic design
From figs and orchids through to rafflesia so fine.
Traffic jams of insects kiss the flowers, consenting to interact
With the notion of continued life as indisputable fact:
An unfailing logic which this forest-universe has never lacked.
While owls fly silently, swifts and hornbills hover above,
All dedicatedly revolving the eternal wheel of love
Which has the strength of an eagle and the peace of a dove.
Amid the richest undergrowth the bearded pig rummages away,
While brave aerobatic squirrels defy the threat of gravity each day
And battalions of monkeys glide through dense trees on their
giggling way.
Meanwhile, cicadas sing for joy. Screaming from their tiny chests
To celebrate the wonders with which their world is blessed;
Freshly tasting the freedoms of the deep-caring forest...

JUDGEMENT DAY

This swirl of breath and life. An ever-changing array for all to see.
Innumerable forms sharing this one ancient forest of true beauty,
From a momentary haze of insects to the oldest and tallest tree.
Every inhabitant helps or is helped. Symbiotically they create
The law of progressive destiny and fully-interlinked fate
From which human beings must learn before it is too late.
And if, brandishing knives, a deadly destroyer should ever arrive,
The citizens shall join together to scream out the joy of being alive
In this universe whose dearest dream is just to survive.

JUDGEMENT DAY

JUDGEMENT DAY

Another Civil War

It's all enough to make you ill...
Whatever war may be, it's not "civil".
And what could be the desperation
Which splits two sides within one nation?

To me violence never makes sense;
Especially when attacking is called defence.
Why can't we use some mental muscle
Instead of always blood and tussle?

The fighting between two sides in one land
Helps us the stupidity to see and understand.
But the lunacy is just the same...
Whatever the scale of this deadly game.

If no more flags were to be unfurled
And we made one nation of all the world,
Then the futility we'd really be seeing
Of fighting between any human beings...

JUDGEMENT DAY

Destination

I have travelled

Far.

Only one place

Held my heart.

Many distant wanderings

And magical former

Wonderings

Led me

Here.

JUDGEMENT DAY

Art

Tin-cans and toilet-brushes entwined together,
"War and Peace" carved on a square inch of leather,
Bird-droppings floating in oil – it may seem quite crude,
Brightly-lit photographs of a bald, dead nude.

Orange walls decorated with small specks of yellow
Created by a bespectacled, grey-haired fellow…
Art comes in so many shapes and forms
And galleries welcome their visitors in swarms.

Is this art? Why not? If it's sincere invention,
Can't any piece truly deserve our attention?
As well as the feeling and reason and passion,
Isn't all art really just a matter of fashion?

So a thousand bricks stand in hexagonal piles,
Quickly raising millions of scornful smiles…
But if it makes us think or question or feel,
Why should every work have universal appeal?

JUDGEMENT DAY

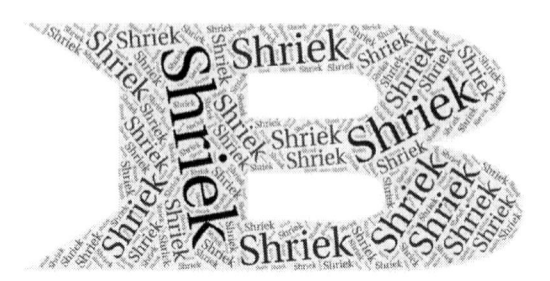

JUDGEMENT DAY

The Shriek

The shriek

Of agony that

Emanates from my soul

For lost friends, missed

Opportunities, broken

Promises, people hurt,

Hours wasted, dreams

Betrayed, love

Unuttered, lies

Told, pain I have

Caused daily

Deafens and drowns

Itself

Out.

JUDGEMENT DAY

What Is Love?

An old question asked and answered

By too many who could care less.

Is it rough, easy, dreamy, real?

Or sense having the sense to feel?

Think less, they say, follow your heart.

What does this confusion reveal?

An unquenched thirst of the soul?

Must we wander and wonder, looking far,

Making battered illusions

Out of tattered delusions

As we hope, one day, for that more

Which gives life to love? Is love hope?

Unclench your heart and let me know.

I know not what, but I hope you so.

JUDGEMENT DAY

A Perfect Life?

Fine shoes, a fine house and a very fast car...
Human evolution has now brought us so far.
Responsible actions? Compassion and such?
No. I'm doing all right, thank you very much.

Build me a house with walls strong and thick.
I'll just ignore reality... It's my cleverest trick.
Protect me from knowledge of every natural form.
I may be ignorant; but I'll stay very warm.

Others may be suffering but I do not care.
There are such difficult problems everywhere.
I may be one of the roots of this poisoned tree,
But I'm sure that it's nothing to do with me...

I'm comfortable enough, safe enough. I am content.
A million excuses for my life I can swiftly invent.
Maybe blinkered, but happy. That's how it should be.
It's simply a case of surviving. It's Me, Me, Me...

JUDGEMENT DAY

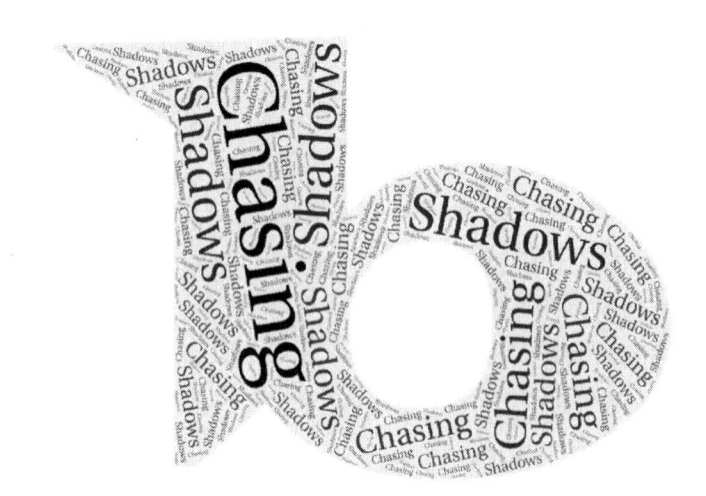

Chasing Shadows

The shadow

Of a cloud

Passes over a mountain,

As a thought

Of you

Passes through my mind.

I climb up

The mountain.

The shadow has gone.

Yet now I have

A clearer view

Of my special cloud

And of all other clouds.

JUDGEMENT DAY

Babies

They burp and they fart and they make lots of noise.
They're silly and small and break all their toys.
They wet their beds - well, what can you do?
Yet people still have babies. I ask you...

They shout for no reason, they're trustful as well.
They break all the rules and they often smell.
They throw up and mess up and laugh at you...
Yet people still have babies. Bizarre, but true.

There must be some urge that we cannot explain
Why people go through those nine months of pain
To be followed by hassle for years upon years
With shouting and torment, trouble and tears.

As they dribble and scream, they fight and kick.
They can break your heart with one naughty trick.
They dirty their clothes and drive you to hell.
Yes, our future's alive... and doing quite well.

JUDGEMENT DAY

Love

Problems are

Questions.

Answers are

Revelations.

Puzzle me your love.

I adore

Your mystery.

JUDGEMENT DAY

The Cage Of Fire

The caged bird shall sing. Its voice shall be heard.
Millions of sympathetic voices shall echo that bird
'Til the cage shall melt in its own futile fire
And the bird will fly free - to guide and inspire.

The search for equal love with sharing and choice
Gave generations of strangers such a passionate voice.
To the world this bird represents a dream come true
Through the life that it's lived and deeds it can do.

Injustice will never be tolerated. We have painfully learned
How the flames of ignorance have too brightly burned.
The world turns so slowly; it must mature until
All spirits can discover their true rights and will.

Let freedom's flames now spread, ablaze with love:
Illuminating all follies, yet still rising above
To light better ways where all promises are kept
Without needlessly causing new tears to be wept.

For freedom must be relished and equally shared;
No-one from its joys should ever be spared.
Each step must be sure - whether big or small,
Until the cage of ignorance is removed from us all.

JUDGEMENT DAY

The Shopper

Another sale is coming around...

Just listen for that dashing sound.

One more offer sending me funny

As I rush off to spend all of my money.

A tea-pot, perhaps. I like to drink to tea.

How useful a Mickey-Mouse-shaped one would be.

I seize every opportunity that brightly glimmers

Of magic toothbrushes and nose-hair trimmers.

But what's this? Someone my joy is halving

By telling me people in the world are starving

And that with some redistribution of our wealth

We could all have houses and all have health.

But I won't ever let them spoil my fun.

Here's the reason I'll protect Number One:

I don't want to be made to live in fear...

And I need to pour tea from Mickey Mouse's ear.

JUDGEMENT DAY

The Candle

As the sun shines,

So the candle burns

When we light

And extinguish it.

Illuminate my heart

With your devoted

Love

And passion.

JUDGEMENT DAY

Developing Nation

The things they accept, it's hard to believe.

The people there must be so naïve...

Some citizens lives so hard they can't cope.

You wonder if their land is beyond all hope.

The political leader controls the army too;

That's military government. It just won't do.

Minorities who rarely share in the ruling...

Fair government? Who d'you think you're fooling?

They destroy the landscape and call it "progress";

While the media lies because of vested interests;

They jail some people with whom they disagree...

It's all simply barbaric if you ask me.

Divisions, absurdity and strangest traditions

Obscure all but the clearest of visions.

Ambitions and dreams are replaced by fear...

Thank goodness none of this happens here.

JUDGEMENT DAY

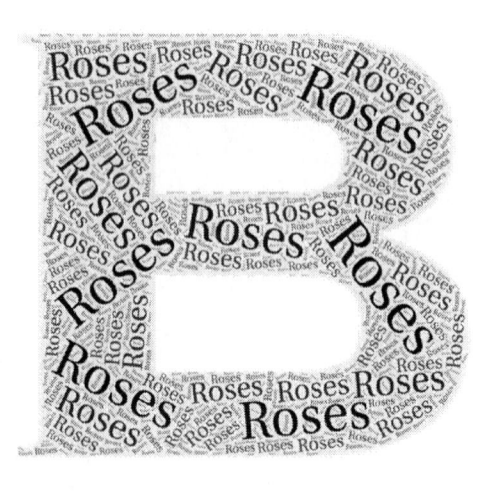

JUDGEMENT DAY

<u>Roses</u>
"How do they know?"
She would say.

He died just after
His fiftieth birthday.

She planted
Fifty rose bushes
In his memory.

Each year
They flowered
For fifty days.

Then,
Like him,
They faded.

"The conifer trees
Are constant and green
All year long,"
She protested.

But
She preferred roses.

JUDGEMENT DAY

JUDGEMENT DAY

The Rhythm of Bali

Night falls. Farmers return home. Dark silence covers
The climbing rice-fields, while riverside lovers
Whisper dreaming hopes that tomorrow may discover.
Suddenly, the timeless rhythm of Bali's drifting clock
Is disturbed by the chiming gecko who repeatedly mocks
The over-rehearsed night-chorus of every frog and cock.
Elsewhere, crashing waves pound the sandy ground,
Recalling the historic rumbles of each volcanic mound,
As distant, simple temples fill with loving, holy sound.
For those with such a mind, the party lights sing bright:
Some select fine dining, while others may scream delight
In neon-covered boxes which shout throughout the night.
But the new day's sun, that ultimate forgiver,
Will, once more, the gentle melody of Bali richly deliver:
With harmonies of palm-trees, groves and life-filled rivers.
Once more the monkeys will commence their joyous play
And deep forests beckon to where ancient mysteries lay,
Revealing the eternal magic of each important day.
Village markets will bustle tunefully, as if trying to outdo
The subtle almost-silence of mountains and endless blue
Which keenly play a part in this island's symphony too.
Sweet notes swim forward everywhere. Your senses lift
As warm air, filled with clove-smoke and incense, drifts
To encounter every spice and flower's richly fragrant gift…

JUDGEMENT DAY

Such union in diversity. Each visitor may swim, sail, climb,
Or relish arts and culture preserved, unstained, by time,
Bathe, relax... even shop. Every excuse here is a rhyme
And reason, as your heart's feelings learn to rest beside
The open smiles that Bali's faces never strive to hide.
Hear the honest melody of laughter from every side.
Immersed, like this, in the glorious music of simple days,
Your heart unburdens, your vision loses care-filled haze,
And you begin to uncover secrets beyond worldly music or phrase...

JUDGEMENT DAY

JUDGEMENT DAY

JUDGEMENT DAY

The Chosen Way

No No No No No No No No
If it's healthy, I don't want to know.
Yes Yes Yes Yes Yes Yes Yes Yes
If it's destructive, give me more not less.

We'll poison the planet and fight with each other;
We'll laugh when we crush any sister and brother;
We'll hoard our belongings, leaving others in need;
We'll plant bombs, not caring where it will lead.

We'll close our eyes to feeling and knowledge;
We'll ignore harmony and burn every bridge;
We'll strike out, cause pain… and then run away;
"Nothing's our fault," is what we will say.

We'll deny all logic - be ignorant instead,
None of it's our problem when we're dead.
Forget about the future. Life's tough – not pretty.
Our chosen way is FUTILITY.

JUDGEMENT DAY

JUDGEMENT DAY

<u>The Martyr</u>
The long shadow
At sunset
Resembles
The shadow at dawn.

Pointing
The other way.

Its darkness
Holds promise
Only

For those willing
To die

For love
For dreams
For others.

And yet
The inevitability
Of the shadow

Holds a warm
And terrible
Devotion.

JUDGEMENT DAY

Nature

A grey shadow silently rests on soft green grass,
A cool breeze – with seeds, sounds, smells – gently drifts past,
A tiger prowls through forests with bright, determined eyes,
A tornado gathers strength in dark, distant skies.

Yet many people ignore all this. Some even succeed…
Locked in prisons of concrete and steel. Where will it lead?
Seeking irrelevance, danger – and not nature's wise heart;
Why should we fear the life-process of which we're a part?

Powerful nature, like unpredictable clockwork, manages all:
Mighty oceans and changing seasons to each insect so small.
Let us acknowledge the forces which we cannot control
And respect and preserve our planet's heart and soul.

We so often play with nature's reflections and trimmings:
Buying flowers, admiring landscapes… maybe go swimming.
Now, let's explore the knowledge that comes from being as one
With those powerful forces of earth, moon and sun…

JUDGEMENT DAY

Logic

It's time
For a New Logic.

Not the logic
Of the gun
And the dollar.

Instead,
The logic
Of a universal bond
Between all people
And between
People and their planet.

The time for this has come.

Such logic
Has been criticised
And ignored.

Now
It must
Be actively pursued.

JUDGEMENT DAY

The Family

So warm a hold, to groom by living gravity,
Silently inspired by each unique unity,
An unbluntable pin to pierce discreetly
And return to some reassured reality.
Such, and for it thanks, is familiarity.

Feelings tap the shoulder of a taller shadow
Filled with dangerous half-dreams of a hero,
Scholar, star, sportsman, sage, saviour,
Inventor, unique initiator... And so,
Familiarly, the effects of gravity grow.

"Perhaps," lives he, "the imagination employs
Polite mirrors, purging this belittlable boy's
Ungrateful, impatient, ignorant insolence,
Undoing talk of feelings, childhood (fragile toys)
Present now in natural, familiar noise."

The anonymous atmosphere that arises
Through deflated deities, surfaced surprises,
Listening, learning, loathing, laughing, loving...
From 'life's core' to 'a ripe fruit's fresh segment' revises.
Thus, sisters, brothers, it familiarises.

JUDGEMENT DAY

Civilisation

The office clock ticks. I do business with (almost) anyone.
I have thick walls, roof and glasses. I hide from the sun.
I have my own rules, ways, books and my very own house,
For I am a human being – not lion, fish or mouse.

I choose friends by accent, status and even by car.
I drink myself quite stupid at my favourite bar.
Politics? I find it all very strange and funny,
I will vote for whoever lets me keep my money.

I have fresh oysters laid out on silver plate,
Served at 8pm – and not half-a-minute late.
I wear designer shoes, watch and expensive shirt,
Drinking best Colombian coffee with Italian dessert.

Civilisation is ceremony – nothing less or more:
Shutting yourself in a room with a thick, bolted door.
Outside world is full of chances… not in my story's text.
All civilisations end. What, I wonder, will come next?

JUDGEMENT DAY

JUDGEMENT DAY

Dream Weaver

Your sport is my work.

I am a trustless

Professional amateur.

Only if you can

Believe or understand

My sunshine and

My shadows and

My moon and my stars

And questionable universe

Will any answer

Come

To you.

Until then,

I cry

Silently.

JUDGEMENT DAY

My Friend

In the woods, a monkey is laughing while at play.
My friend says: "A nice way to spend your day…
This mammal sleeps, then rises each morning.
What will his day bring? There can be no warning.

He eats, washes and plays. And when it gets late
He rushes all around looking for a mate.
His work is survival – trying to do his best,
Each surprising day is a constant test.

But he's not idle. Busy with family and being alive,
Productive in his world – not just from nine to five.
And whenever it rains he is not quite so merry…
It makes it harder to seek out leaf and berry.

He means no harm. Sometimes, it must be said,
He does things he'll regret 'til the day he's dead.
He aims to live with some pleasure and not much fuss."
Is this monkey different from any or all of us?

JUDGEMENT DAY

Habit

Habit

Grips our neck

Like a

Frustrated nun.

JUDGEMENT DAY

JUDGEMENT DAY

For -

Destiny led me to your eyes...
Your eyes smiled at me,
Making my heart bleed with tears of flame
Which ignited the love in my soul.

Other sparks had formerly flown
To singe the corners of my hopes,
Warming and pushing me forward;
Preparing me for this true fire.

Only you held the absolute magic
To make me fully burn.

And, though this bright fire
Shows no ways or answers
Or where this feeling will grow,
I have no fears.

For I believe with absolute love
That you are the only certainty
I need or want or shall ever desire to know.
I trust our joyful dreams

As I blissfully abseil
Into the blazing abyss
Of absolute love
With you.

JUDGEMENT DAY

JUDGEMENT DAY

When? Where? How?

Is this our moment? Is this the right hour
To find the true potential of people power?
Who makes the rules? Can we have our say?
Is it sorrow for tomorrow or success from today?

Look around. Beyond shiny surface and fashion,
And relish the gift of feeling compassion.
Sad wrongs have continued for too long,
People must unite their power – pure and strong.

Feeling everyone's pain, sensing every joy too,
Considering the effect of all that you do…
Each child your child, each adult your sister or brother;
It's not one law for you, and another for every other.

The process has started. Every voice shall be heard.
Delivering through action – not just well-chosen words.
This is not some philosophy in a book on a shelf…
And to change the world, you must start with yourself.

JUDGEMENT DAY

JUDGEMENT DAY

<u>Yesterday</u>
Upon our shoulders
We carry gold.
In our ways
We display dirt.

Getting gold from dirt
Is difficult
And takes many
Many years.

But please, buy
No mud.
Respect
No shit-sellers.

Out of dirt
Make
Perfect
Invisible statues

Which will shine
Like gold.

JUDGEMENT DAY

JUDGEMENT DAY

The Village

The sun rises. Each peaceful dwelling contains
A helpful, sharing family. Nothing remains
Of competition which destroys more than creates.
Let's move back to villages – before it's too late.

Everyone receiving according to need and worth,
No-one included or excluded by wealth or birth.
Let highways and skyscrapers yield to natural charms,
As we turn away from ignorance and deadly arms.

Even cities can divide into segments for now,
Living in harmony while working out how
Into the arms of nature to safely return –
To live creatively and not to kill and burn.

Fights and destruction have divided us too long.
Working together will make us all more strong…
Until the villages melt and each human stands tall
As a truly fulfilled and knowing animal.

JUDGEMENT DAY

JUDGEMENT DAY

<u>Now</u>

The dinosaurs

Laid down,

Becoming mountains.

The gods

Acquiesced

And became ideas.

Our hopes

Mellowed

To certain joy.

Our fears

Grew

To hatred.

And so everything

Must change

Until

The dinosaurs roam again.

JUDGEMENT DAY

JUDGEMENT DAY

The Volcano

A gash in the mountain, a bleeding wound
Roared with life... The travellers swooned.
A tear in the earth, revealing the heart;
The universe screaming - as it did at the start.
The waves of fire leap, rush and roar,
Waiting for compassion from our hearts to pour...
Seeing wasted hours, destruction and shame,
Calling our stupidity by its own name.
For we built illusions, saying: "Each must find
A way to excuse their dissatisfied mind."
We ignore miracles and beauty, great sounds and joy;
Treating our home and master like a disposable toy.

You may be more tolerant than I.
I can't watch people watch their lives go by
Without saying: "Look. There's a better way.
Let's make a difference and make it today.
We are animals. Part of nature. That and no more.
So listen now to the waves' bright roar...
Respect all nature, love, wisdom and truth,
Those simple joys we felt in our youth."
And what's that sound we hear every day
That we just shrug off or explain away?
It's waves of fire rushing through our soul
Burning with the need for us to be whole.

JUDGEMENT DAY

Money

A child is told: "If you're good, here's a penny."

So the child grows up wanting to have many.

People love riches – now isn't it funny?

They'll do anything to have pockets full of money.

The rich laugh at poor; the poor can't reply.

Some people for money would fight and die.

We get divided and work against each other...

For a million dollars, would you kick your grandmother?

Money was invented to help trade - nothing more;

Like toy counters to exchange for goods at the store.

But it's been so distorted - with a wink and a nod;

Until it is worshipped like some almighty god.

Money causes division, snobbery and fights.

Wealth is not the same as worth or as rights.

Can't we end this futility, find some logic instead?

Exchange the religion of money for sense - in our hearts and heads.

ered letter B filled with the word "Newborn"

Newborn

Your glittering eyes

Surprised by newness

Are somehow old.

The knowledge you bring

And will soon forget

Is the inexplicable

You will spend

The rest of your life

Trying to understand.

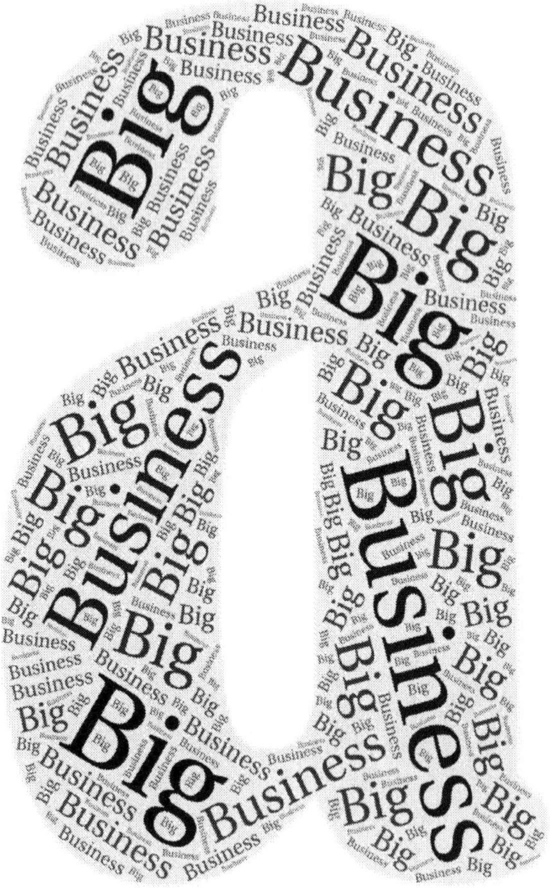
Big
Business

Big Business

I'm not a criminal... I'm a businessperson.
You can tell by the accent with which I'm conversin'.
You can tell by my suit - so expensive and clean,
By my briefcase, my 'phone, my coffee machine.

I'm dignified, not a conman. Let's state the facts.
I'm merely *creative* with all my profits and tax.
Relieving people of their money? I never miss...
But everyone knows that's just good business.

Some people may suffer - disaster, death, divorces,
While I make fortune... but that's market forces.
I don't lie, I persuade - it's within the law.
The losers are at fault. Business is just like war.

My status allows me to do what I'm wishin',
I've many a good friend who's a politician...
My profits are made through cleverness, not scams.
My designer shoes show how respectable I am...

JUDGEMENT DAY

Teenagers

When others think

They

Are at their worst,

They think

They

Are at their best.

It was ever thus.

Thanks be.

JUDGEMENT DAY

JUDGEMENT DAY

<u>Dawn</u>

With breakfast in bed on my birthday,
Came a sense of my spirit being renewed.
The coffee was made her own special way:
Sweetened, microwaved and overstewed.

I realised that I was not dreaming;
Something real was happening here.
The resurrection of my soul's singing,
Drowning out tiredness, trouble and fear.

My spirit was low, my heart was dragging;
Dreams were dark that once seemed bright.
She gave me hope, set my thoughts winging
With love by day, sweet love by night.

Such summer lights filled the nights,
We laughed and played away the day.
Finding something that felt so right,
The renewal of friendship far away.

The brightness of a new beginning,
Bringer of hope when I was forlorn,
The light that came when sight was dimming:
My definition of a dawn.

JUDGEMENT DAY

To The Politician

"Tomorrow will be different!" you yesterday cried,
"We'll make bad things better!" ...but you lied.
For still injustice, inequality and deepest hurt
Inhabit your hypocrisy's barren desert...

You gave a token. A token. A symbol so mild.
You helped one group find work. You fed one child.
Don't do us any favours... In humanity's name
Dare to make a difference. Forget about your fame.

True change, not tinkering, is what we seek;
Flesh out the grand words with which you speak.
Grasp those difficulties, pull them out by the root,
Before even more hopes get trampled underfoot.

Don't do us any favours - pathetic and small.
What will our grandchildren say of us all?
Tinkering gets you through today and tomorrow;
Truly acting prevents our grandchildren's sorrow.

JUDGEMENT DAY

<u>Elephants</u>
Elephants ran in the desert,
Thinking:
'What are we doing here?'
Elephants ran in the desert,
Wishing
Some water was near.

The storyteller said to the elephants:
"Dream of
Flying, if you dare."
Their ears flapped, their trunks swung
And they dreamt
Of being elsewhere.

Elephants ran in the desert.
But now
A home they have found,
Because they dared to fly
On the breeze
Of the story's sound.

And we are lighter than elephants.
That is
A fact we know.
Find your dream, flap your wings,
Take to
The air and go...

JUDGEMENT DAY

Sex

Sex is simply bad. Sex is just shoddy.
You shouldn't be allowed to enjoy your body.
It's a very clear rule... not made by me...
Sex was never a part of our destiny.

It's something new, this whole sex craze thing.
Our terrible generation brought it all in...
Just ask yourselves and then ask each other:
Was there sex between your father and mother?

I confess that sometimes I feel like it too...
I've simply been told that it's bad and it's blue.
If I go down that path then it is for sure
I'll become an ordinary mortal of nature.

So I will keep telling you that it's a sin
When I don't like the hole that you're putting it in.
Sex only brings heartache and the occasional sore.
So it must all end. Enjoy sex no more!

JUDGEMENT DAY

JUDGEMENT DAY

<u>And Now</u>

The impossible waits

Patiently

For us

To discover

The reason why

It is possible.

JUDGEMENT DAY

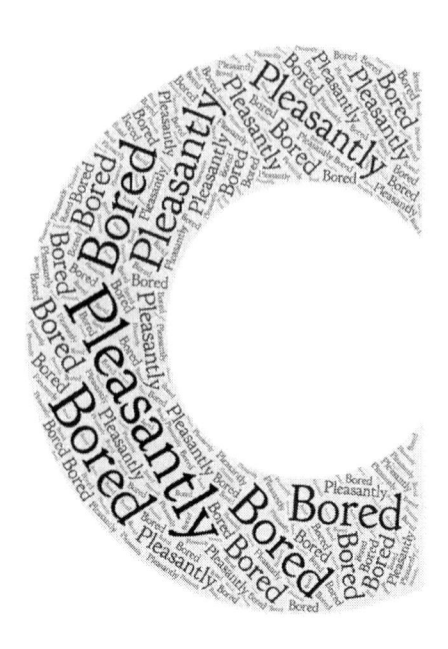

Pleasantly Bored

When I was young, I ran every mile,
And I said everything with a smile.
Now for the first time since I was born,
I'm taking it slow, learning to yawn...

I'm achieving a state I think is great,
Learning to live before it's too late.
Finding peace of mind, never known the kind,
And who knows what I may now find...

Dreams at night once made me cry,
Wanting it all – for tomorrow I die.
Plans were what I used to swear by,
But things come easier now I don't try.

Been too many ways to too many places,
Told too many lies to too many faces.
Now I do something I always ignored...
Taking the time to be pleasantly bored.

So have I given up? You bet your life NOT!
I still make the most of the chances I've got.
I still climb mountains with all of my powers,
But now I stop to smell the flowers...

Because I've learned one thing I never knew:
It's not *how much* but *what* you do.

JUDGEMENT DAY

Question and Answer

What's it all about? Us, once again becoming a part
Of nature. That will be our planet's best new start.
We must work towards this with each thought and action;
United and peaceful... not divided into factions.

How will we? Well, this will be our special task:
Examine the heart of everything. Ignore each useless mask.
The heart of nature lives inside our hearts too,
Respect this reality in everything we do.

The journey may be long. And yet together we'll go,
With each move and action making us grow
More sure and more calm... as each human being
Seeks out the true heart of all they are seeing.

Reject futility and destruction. Remember, after all,
In the global picture we are each very small.
And, once again, we'll be a part of and not apart from
This beautiful universe that is our home.

JUDGEMENT DAY

Dreams

Dancing and playing

Within thoughts untold.

Remembering, foretelling

The new and the old.

All coloured with

Gleams and sunbeams,

Anything can occur

In the country of dreams.

Meaning and illusion

Mingle to reveal

Shadows and whispers

Of everything real.

JUDGEMENT DAY

New World

Can we end selfish destruction that we've been seeing
And put some humanity back into human being?
Can we seek views and solutions of different sorts,
Welcoming and embracing radical new thoughts?

Let's find short-term changes to create long-term gain;
Ending selfish futility and starting to alleviate pain.
The plan for the future could employ ancient ideas
Like co-operation, to reduce human and animal tears.

'Reduce, Reuse, Recycle' is a such familiar phrase,
Yet it could hold the instructions to guide our ways:
Reduce destruction. Reuse true sense. Recycle and share.
Evolving to a new understanding of mutual care.

What sort of future should our children be forced to face?
Is there an opportunity, now, that we can embrace?
Fashioned through compassion and ignoring all scorn,
We'll be rewarded by the lives of generations unborn…

JUDGEMENT DAY

Two Rules

There are only two rules.

Firstly

'Stop the rot'.

Hurt no-one more,

Do no more damage.

Secondly

'Start the repair'.

Help whoever you can,

Begin working towards

An ever closer union

With the fellow occupants

Of your planet

And the planet itself.

The time to do this

Is right now.

JUDGEMENT DAY

JUDGEMENT DAY

One Nation

"Welcome to the new day, a new world and to countless
beautiful feelings unknown.
Taste our clean air. Relish the rewards of the pure, natural food
we are daily shown,"
Said the father to the son... but in a language very different
from our own:
Simpler, apparently unformed, yet deeper; less intricate, yet
infinitely more loving and true.
As he spoke, the sun blinked over green hills into skies
of fresh and clearest blue
And every animal stirred and lived - making every
old acquaintance breathe anew.
"For it was not always like this," said the father. "Our ancestor humans
roamed this very place
Uprooting its beauty and harmony - replacing it all with destruction
and disgrace;
And hardly a moment of shame cast its dark shadow over
their proudly defiant face.
They believed that life was a mystery, death was defeat and simplicity
was a crime.
They avoided questions that needed answers. They preferred
to spend their time
Manufacturing their own problems to solve. That way, their self-esteem
could climb

JUDGEMENT DAY

As they constantly congratulated themselves on their absurd divisions
and dangerous ideas.

They denied everything beyond their own creation... ignoring all
the reality, sharp and clear,

That screamed out all around - in nature, in their souls and in every
love so dear.

Slowly, however, things changed. Science as Ruler was disproved -
wisely, it was revealed

To be an incomplete recipe for a dish that was already formed.
Our wounds healed

When we chose, instead, simply to taste the perfect dish and to fully
emotionally yield.

We renounced all war and futility; we became a willing part of
everything around;

We made our homes grow out of - and not destroy - our ancient
mother ground;

And we newly listened to the bleating, bleeding wisdom of every
plant and animal's sound.

Firstly, we were brave and moved back to villages - forgoing
the concrete and steel of our misspent youth.

We pursued, once more, a union between our existence and all
undeniable knowledge and truth;

No longer would we attack our own heart and soul with
a falsely sharpened tooth...

JUDGEMENT DAY

Eventually, the villages melted. We became, simply, one of the animals.
Our newly-washed eyes
Discovered to their eternal shame and constantly rewarded,
uniquely delighted surprise
That compassion and harmony brought the wise benefits
that no-one now denies.
We learned that true knowledge and feeling are life. We freed ourselves,
beginning to heal
The wounds that many would not even admit they had. Everything
that is deep and real
Re-entered our hearts and minds. We recreated a union, like the spokes
of a single wheel,
With every detail of our universe. Our planet began to heal. We made
peace with each other.
Every animal and perfect creation became our once-again certain
sister and brother
In a delighted and daily celebration of our joint One Nation.
We need no other."

JUDGEMENT DAY

ABOUT THE AUTHOR

Judge The Poet has been a professional writer and performer of poetry, all around the world, for more than three decades.

He currently lives in the middle of England, with his partner and their two children.

Printed in Great Britain
by Amazon